"No ideas but in things."
WILLIAM CARLOS WILLIAMS

JESUS WITH DIRTY FEET

A DOWN-TO-EARTH LOOK AT CHRISTIANITY FOR THE CURIOUS & SKEPTICAL

DON EVERTS

InterVarsity Press
Downers Grove, Illinois

InterVarsity Press

P.O. Box 1400, Downers Grove, IL 60515
World Wide Web: www.ivpress.com
E-mail: mail@ivpress.com

InterVarsity Press® is the book-publishing division of InterVarsity Christian Fellowship/USA®, a student movement active on campus at hundreds of universities, colleges and schools of nursing in the United States of America, and a member movement of the International Fellowship of Evangelical Students. For information about local and regional activities, write Public Relations Dept., InterVarsity Christian Fellowship/USA, 6400 Schroeder Rd., P.O. Box 7895, Madison, WI 53707-7895.

References to and paraphrases of Scripture are in the author's own words.

Cover design: Cindy Kiple
Cover image: Hans Neleman/Photonica

ISBN 0-8308-2206-2

Printed in the United States of America ♾

Library of Congress Cataloging-in-Publication Data has been requested.

Everts, Don, 1971-
  Jesus with dirty feet: a down-to-earth look at Christianity for
the curious and skeptical/Don Everts.
         p.   cm.
  Includes bibliographical references.
  ISBN 0-8308-2206-2 (pbk. : alk. paper)
  1. Christianity.   I. Title.
BR121.2.E935   1999
230—dc21
                                                                      99-21815
                                                                      CIP

P	23	22	21	20	19	18	17	16	15	14	13
Y	16	15	14	13	12	11	10	09	08	07	06

Contents

Introduction

Here at the dawn of a new millennium we may be postmodern, but we are certainly not post-brain cells.

It may seem unlikely, given the superficial, breakneck pace of life these days, but we are—quite vigorously—curious and thoughtful creatures. We ask questions. We ponder meaning and truth. We think deeply.

Call it a lapse into philosophy, call it spirituality, call it too much caffeine. Whatever. The fact is, despite the unending barrage of everyday life, many of us simply can't help but think and wonder and contemplate the deeper things in life.

For some of us that wondering eventually gets around to Jesus and Christianity. We wonder if it's really as inspiring as some say—or as idiotic as others insist. So we start to ask our own questions. Who was Jesus? Did he really say anything worth listening to? Is there anything to this Christian religion that he started?

But trying to get clear answers about Jesus is a bit tricky, because everyone and their dog has a different opinion about Jesus.

Let's see . . . there's the traditional stained-glass Jesus, my grandparents' soft Jesus who blesses nice people who don't smoke or cuss, the liberationists' machine-gun-toting Jesus, the atheists' papier-mâché Jesus—not to mention the Republican Jesus, the liberal Jesus, the finger-wagging Jesus, the limp-wristed Jesus . . .

You can see the problem.

We could just throw up our hands in frustration at all the

conflicting caricatures. Or I suppose we could just let others spoon-feed us some prechewed conclusions about him. But life's too short for all that. There must be a way to make up our own minds.

Well, maybe there is. The great American poet William Carlos Williams insisted that the truest source of clarity is the tangible. Theory, rhetoric and dogmatism only mislead, cloud and confuse. "No ideas but in things," he said. True clarity of thought comes from "things," the tangible and specific and touchable in life.

If Williams was right, then clarity about Jesus will come not from preconceived notions and theories *about* him but from a simple, clear, specific look at Jesus himself.

But is that even possible? Is it possible to see Jesus without all the clichés and stereotypes that have piled up over the last two thousand years? Can we wipe away some of the gloss of twenty centuries and see Jesus tangibly and in detail, as those first folks on the streets of Israel saw him . . . dirty feet and all?

Well, this simple book is an attempt to do that, to peel back the centuries by going back to the very first accounts of Jesus. What did he do? What did he say? What was he really like?

Instead of relying on complex theologies for answers, this book looks to the words of Jesus himself and the earliest accounts of his life. I hope we'll be able to side-step most of the intervening clichés, assumptions and rhetoric that have accumulated over the last two thousand years.

I've written it down in what are called "sense lines." This way of writing is nothing new or fancy but something very old and simple. The ancients used this way of writing (*per cola et commata,* they called it) to help them contemplate what they were reading.

By illustrating parallel thoughts, isolating key words and

putting into greater relief the development of ideas, sense lines help us to slowly chew on the distinct ideas present— to weigh and judge ideas instead of just blindly swallowing or instinctively spitting out everything. I figured that in this hectic day and age that old idea might not be such a bad one.

Well, with all that said, let's leave behind the bulky, vague legacy of two thousand years of stereotypes and clichés and venture back to the beginning. Then, like the people Jesus met in his own day, we'll be able to see him for ourselves.

1
Christianity
Smelly Fishermen

Most folks think Christianity is
an outdated religion.

But it turns out it is neither outdated
nor a religion.

The Beginning: "Follow Me"

It is safe to say
that when most of us read the word *Christianity*
we really read "Religious Institution"

or "Crusty, Old, Outdated, Arrogant Religious Institution"
for that matter.

> Images flash into our minds:

>> everything from the Crusades to
>> the perpetually complex and powerful
>> Vatican machinery to two millennia of
>> steeples and pews and organs to
>> cheesy, makeup-laden
>> televangelists who want our money.

> That, we say, is "Christianity."

>> A religious institution—
>> and a bad one at that.

Surprisingly,
when the word was first coined
it referred to something much more
simple and provocative and shocking.

> To really understand
> "Christianity"
>> we have to go back to the beginning,
>> to put first things first.

For starters, Jesus was not a Christian.

He never asked anyone to become a Christian,
    never built a steepled building,
    never drew up a theological treatise,
    never took an offering,
    never wore religious garments,
    never incorporated for tax purposes . . .

He simply called people to follow him.

That's it.
        That, despite its simplicity,
        is it.

He called people to follow him.

    The first two were brothers:
    Simon and Andrew.

    Regular guys.
        Simple fishermen.
            The first two Christians ever.

    Those brothers didn't think at all
    about "becoming Christians"
    or taking on a new religion.

        Here was this thirty-year-old man
        (a carpenter)
        who simply said "follow me."

    And they believed him.

So, in faith,
these two brothers

gave their lives to him
(literally),

putting down
their familiar nets
and following him.

Here was the birthplace
of a way of life,
of a reality
that would change the world forever.

Before hurrying on
with words
and centuries
of theology,   we must pause

at the cradle
of what we call Christianity.

It is never more
than Jesus' call: "Follow me"

and a response: dropping familiar nets

and following, in faith,
this sandaled Jewish man.

It is never more than that.

Two thousand years of words can do nothing
to the simple, basic reality of Christianity:

Those first steps

taken by those two brothers.
Simon and Andrew's theology
was as pure as it gets:

"Jesus said, 'Follow me.' And we did."

This is the only starting place.

Presumption and pride
    in the cathedral grandness
        and stained-glass intricacy
            of two thousand years of Reigning Religion
must not fabricate a Christianity that is too eloquent
for its simple beginnings.

Simon and Andrew
are Christianity's blue-collar
            dirty-finger
                patriarchs

(who probably never quite shook that smell of fish).

They are where this thing called "Christianity" begins,
    and where
    our understanding of it
    must begin.

* * * *

A Band of Followers

As Jesus went about his amazing business,
people responded to him in various ways.
    Many (great crowds of wide-eyes)

became intrigued
by him and his healings and miracles.

Some (the ruling tribes)
became dead-set against
him and his teachings.

But a few (hearing something undeniable in his call)
left their lives to walk with him.

People solemnly mention this last group
(in hushed tones) as

"The Disciples of Jesus."

But *disciple* just means *follower.*
And there was nothing solemn
about these first Jesus Followers:

several fishermen,
a tax man,
a revolutionary guerrilla,
a lawyer . . .

men and women who left their homes
to walk some dust-covered streets
in a small section of the Middle East
all because they believed Jesus.

What we would call "Christianity"
was nothing more
and nothing less
than some simple people
responding to Jesus' call

by attaching themselves to him.

They believed,
    followed,
        listened to,
            questioned,
                obeyed,
                    talked with,
                        learned from
    and ultimately gave their lives to
    this character Jesus.

That
is Christianity.

* * * *

The Tribe That Never Ends

This following of Jesus
    proved to be such a thrilling adventure,
    proved to be so worth it,

        that the initial Jesus Followers
        couldn't help but tell others all about it!

It had really been news to them,
    and so once they realized
    just how good that news really was,
        they just *had* to tell someone else.

So this first band of followers
started telling others about following Jesus
        and when those folks believed and started following

they too couldn't help but tell others
and so on and so forth
until we get to those Jesus Followers

who live next door to us today.

When that small band
became a much larger crowd

people had to refer to them somehow.

So folks started calling them

"People of the Way."

Their "way" was
to abandon themselves
to following this Jesus

who they unflinchingly believed
was the long-awaited Messiah
that their people had been waiting for
for centuries.

And since the Greeks
translated the word *Messiah*
as *Christ*

folks started calling
the Jesus Followers
"Christ-ones" or
"Christ-ians"   as it ended up
getting put.

And it seems that's the name that stuck

    So "Christian-ity"   is simply the word
                           folks coined
                           to refer to these Christ-ians
                           and all their adventures.

Plain old Christianity:

    not a set of dogmatic principles,
    not a life philosophy,
    not an outdated old religious institution,
    but a peculiar band of people—

that group of followers
    that's been on the move
        for the past two thousand years,
            busy doggedly following
                this Jesus.

When you see "Christianity,"

read, *The Never-Ending Adventures and Journeys
    of the Jesus Followers.*

2
Jesus
God's Dirty Feet

Most folks think of Jesus as the man who started that Christianity religion.

But it turns out he wasn't just a man, and he wasn't interested in religion.

The Key to Christianity

Jesus isn't the proud founding father of Christianity.
He isn't even the patron saint of Christianity.

> If Christianity
> (*The Adventures of the Jesus Followers*)
> > is nothing more than
> > the story of folks literally following Jesus,

> > then Jesus defines,
> > > determines
> > > > and creates
> > *The Adventures of the Jesus Followers*
> > > with his every step,
> > > > with his every posture,
> > > > > with each teaching
> > > > > > and each "follow me"
> > > > > > > he speaks to his followers.

If Jesus had created an institution,
we could ask about it,
> look at it,
> > examine it.
> > > But he didn't.
> > > He simply called people
> > > to follow him.

> So, if we want to know anything about
> *The Adventures of the Jesus Followers,*

> > we have to start with Jesus.

We must ask about him,

look at him,
examine his words.

He is the point of the whole thing.
He is the center.

Catching even a brief, clear glimpse of Jesus himself
must be our priority
        if we have any hopes
        of coming to any conclusions about
The Adventures of the Jesus Followers.

*   *   *   *

The Life of Jesus

Jesus' first thirty years or so
were spent as a carpenter and masonry worker.

    Then, after being baptized
    by his hairy cousin John,

        Jesus walked out into the wilderness
        without food or shelter.

        He stayed for a few weeks
            in that remote,
            barren wilderness.

        The ruling spiritual powers tempted him
            with the gift
                of enduring,
                    unimaginable
                        political power . . .

but Jesus,
tired and hungry and alone,
did not relent.

He had something very different in mind.

Having resisted the temptation,
having resolved his purpose with clarity . . .

Jesus walked back into town

and changed the world forever.

He had emerged ready for a very different life.

His neighbors and family were shocked.
Complete strangers were enthralled.
Large crowds sought him out.

And the ruling religious leaders were
dumbfounded and panicked.

He was like nothing anyone had ever seen.

Among a people that smugly shunned
the sick and ill,

Jesus stopped,
looked beggars in the eyes,
touched lepers,
and brought dignity to the helpless and alone.

In a day of religion-for-profit
and jockeying for religious merit and prestige,

Jesus condemned
the injustices of the powerful
and affirmed
the simple, true faith of the poor.

In the midst of a cloudy landscape
of moral compromise,

Jesus brightly declared
the reality of sin.

In his actions
and teachings
and conversations
and relationships
Jesus was entirely different and new and stunning.

There was just something so clear
and beautiful
and true
and unique
and powerful about Jesus

that old rabbis would marvel at his teachings,
young children would run up and sit in his lap,
ashamed prostitutes would find themselves
weeping at his feet,
whole villages would gather
to hear him speak,
experts in debate of the law
would find themselves
speechless,

and people from the poor

to the rugged working class
    to the unbelievably wealthy
would leave everything . . . to follow him.

Nothing would ever be the same
after Jesus embarked on those three
absolutely unique years.

Jesus walked and taught and healed.

Jesus walked.

Jesus was a man with dirty feet.

He spent most of those three years
walking around with people.

    He invited folks to become
    his intimate followers.

    Everywhere he went
    great crowds gathered around
    to listen to him,
        to be with him,
            to see what he would do next.

As Jesus led his twelve closest followers
they would walk along the dirt roads together.

    They went to parties together.
    They ate meals together.
    They worked together.
Jesus walked as a human among humans,

brushed elbows with politicians and outcasts,
went to parties with
sinners and criminals,
and embraced as his own family
those he met on the street.

Jesus floated on no pristine clouds.

Jesus was no aloof elitist.

Jesus was no odd hermit.

He preferred the world of

dirt and friends and handshakes.

He embraced this relational life on earth
more passionately than anyone ever had.

Jesus taught.

His favorite topic was the Kingdom of God.

But Jesus wasn't like other teachers of his day.

He never spoke vaguely
with some esoteric code language.

He never obfuscated
with intellectual, theological terms.

He never used convoluted traps
to trick people into looking foolish.

Jesus spoke in the language of parables.

Using crystal-clear metaphors
and provocatively simple stories

Jesus described what the Kingdom was like.

His most impassioned speeches
were no more than

common agricultural truisms,

basic stories about seeds
and manure
and sheep,

innocent stories
laced with razor-sharp truth.

Like barbed fishhooks,
Jesus' simple words
seemed to find their way
— permanently—
into people's souls.

His truth, uncomfortable for some
and a balm for others,

was always stunningly clear
and its implications always unavoidable.

The debaters of the day
soon stopped trying to trick Jesus.
He just wouldn't play their games.

His teaching illumined the mysteries of life,
     nailed the realities of human nature,
       spoke clearly of God's ways
         and brightly proclaimed the news
          of the Kingdom and its possibilities.

People in great crowds pressed in
to get close enough to hear his words.

   And they were left standing
either indignant or thoughtfully silent

     when he finished.

He taught like no one ever had.

And Jesus healed.

The sick,
the outcasts,
the possessed,
the marginalized
and the suffering   were attracted to Jesus,
              sought him out,
              found healing in him.

   He touched lepers,
   ate with social outcasts,
   listened to the cries of the ignored . . .

     and healings abounded!

It was as if his touch were the touch of God.

Illnesses,
  evil spirits,
    social stigmas,
      loneliness,
        fatal diseases,

          even death itself

        seemed simply to disappear
        at his touch.

    No one could explain these healings.
    And no one could stop talking about them.

    Jesus healed in ways no one ever had.

Now, these weren't public relations healings.
    No PR moves.

        Jesus told those he healed
        to keep it to themselves.
        "Just between you and me."

        He wasn't trying to win
        political favors. He cared.

    In fact, Jesus demonstrated
    a distinct disinterest in politics,
        wasting no time
        trying to impress the establishment
        or pander to the powerful.

You see, Jesus' popularity rarely extended to those in charge.
    The religious leaders,

the politicians,
the Keepers of the Status Quo
   were all threatened by him:
     his walking,
      his teaching,
       his healing . . .
the tide of changing lives that he was creating.

So they drew up a tidy plan
and tried to kill him.
And that's when things got really interesting.
   You see, Jesus *let* them kill him.
   And then he didn't stay dead.

Shocking, indeed. It silenced everyone.

And one thought
   was left on the lips
     and in the heart
      of everyone for thousands of miles
      and hundreds of years:

    Who is this Jesus?

   * * * *

Jesus the "I Am"

The ancient Israelites were strange.

   They insisted that there was only one God
   and that they knew this because he came to them
      and told them so.

When they asked him his name he said,
  "I am who I am"

  or "I will be what I will be."
  (Translators are still trying
  to figure that one out!)

The "I Am" for short.
"Yahweh" in their language.

As his name would suggest,
this God was quite absolutely unlike
any other gods ever heard of.

  All their neighbors
  had simple statue gods,
    little carved bulls,
      fashioned fertility dolls.

  But the "I Am" . . . well, he actually talked
                          and acted
                          and cared.

And to top it all off,
this Yahweh claimed to have created all things.

  Yahweh.

  Not some small carved god-of-olive-trees.
  Not a fashioned stone god-of-rain.

The one God.
The only God.
The "capital G" God.

The "I Am."

This Yahweh was so powerful
and real
and tangible
that just laying eyes on him could kill you.

Those tough, desert-hardened Israelites
even stopped daring to pronounce his name!

The "I Am" is that awe-inspiring.

And here's the kicker about Jesus:
He claimed he was this Yahweh . . . in person!

The "I Am" Creator who fashioned the whole universe
had done the most shocking thing:

He enfleshed himself.

No James-Earl-Jones-Booming-Voice-from-the-Clouds.

No.

Jesus said he was God   up close,
a word
whispered
intimately
in our ears.

Jesus was God
speaking words
no one could have
imagined.

Jesus,
The Intimate Word. The Close One.
Jesus,
The ancient Hebrew Yahweh who breathes
and talks
and loves.

That unassuming carpenter with dusty sandals
was the very one who thought up and created
that dust clinging to his sandals.

* * * *

Jesus the "Anointed One"

"That Day."

The ancient Israelites
always whispered in their tents at night about
That Day.

Young boys and girls
exchanged stories
their parents had told them about
That Day.

Old, leathered men
would slowly stroke their beards
wondering if That Day would come
before their own days came to an end.

For generation upon generation
the Hebrews had been waiting for
That Day—

the blessed day
when *he* would come!
The Anointed One, that is.

On That Day,
the "I Am's" saving presence would come in person
as the One who was special,
who was anointed.
The One to save.
The One to heal.
The One to suffer—but win.

They waited for the promised Anointed One
or *Messiah,* as their language spoke it.

They knew he would come.
The only question was when.

Through beatings in slavery they waited.

In prison camps far from their destroyed homes
they waited.

Even while prospering in times of victory,
they waited.

And then one day
in a dirty barn
he came.

The nation erupted! *He* had come!
The intricate prophecies were exactly fulfilled!
The cosmos changed forever!

The Messiah . . . he had finally come!

It was just as it had always been promised.

It was first-century Israel,
and the man who caused all the commotion
was none other than Jesus himself.

"They say his name is Jesus,"
        they would whisper to each other
        as they rushed to the synagogue
        to hear him teach.

                Little boys and girls would squeal
                when Jesus (the Messiah!) would stop
                to talk with them and hold them.

                And when Jesus was still a tiny baby,
                one old man,
                a complete stranger named Simeon,
                        stopped stroking his beard
                        when he saw the baby, Jesus.

                He walked over,
                picked Jesus up with his old,
                wrinkled hands and
                        (as Jesus' mother
                        watched with wonder)
                held him up toward the sky.

        Simeon thanked God
        that he could finally die in peace,
        for he had lived to see That Day.

The Messiah had finally come.

* * * *

In His Own Words

Jesus' lengthy inaugural address, his coming-out speech, his summary of his entire message, how he kicked off those three years:

> "I've got some good news for you . . .
> The Kingdom of Yahweh has come near!
>
> You can turn around now."

Jesus' rallying cry, his campaign strategy, his insightful and persuasive rhetoric:

> "Follow me."

Jesus on himself:

> "I am bread—
>   you are starving,
>   and I am life-saving bread.
>
>   I am your sustenance,
>   the basic staple you need to live.
>   If you eat me
>   you will live.
>
> I am light.
>   You are stumbling in darkness,
>   and I am illuminating light.

If you follow me
you'll stop stubbing your souls.

I am a shepherd.
You are ill-fated, awkward,
short-sighted animals,
and I am
your loving shepherd.
I've named you.
I really like you.
I lead you to feasts of grass
and kill the scheming wolves.

You know my voice
and will live as you follow it.

I am a vine.
You are little branches,
and I am the only vine
that reaches the ground
and has roots in the rich soil.

If you don't anchor yourself in me,
you will be a brittle, dead branch.

If you make a home in me,
you will bear fruit.
That's the whole point of a branch.

I am your father.
You are my beautiful children,
and I am your provider
and forgiving comforter.

If you live with me,
you'll grow up
in strength and wisdom.

You'll grow up
in the freedom of knowing
you're always loved and treasured.

Jesus the Messiah's intricate, well-thought-out strategy
for ultimate victory, his game plan, his secret weapon, his
plan of attack that would change reality forever:

"I'll tell everyone the good news
about turning around . . .

and then those in charge
will want to see me dead.

And they will . . . for three days.

And after those three days
we will have turned a corner.

Reality will be indelibly altered.

I will have beaten death.

And we will have won.
Forever."

* * * *

The Plan

You see, the most powerful thing happened:

> Jesus didn't stay dead.
> After three days he was alive again,
> to the amazement of his disciples
> and the dumb-struck he passed on the road.

It was as he had always said it would be:
death proved as simple an obstacle as leprosy.

> By letting his enemies kill him
> and then rising from his tomb
> > Jesus had accomplished the impossible:

> He defeated death.

> And in that one act he wiped out   sin,
> > > > > guilt,
> > > > > regret,
> > > > > penalty.

> In his unprecedented,
> unquestionable act

> Jesus had changed reality forever.

Those who (jaws hanging open) saw Jesus alive again
> found themselves breathing:
> > "He really is bread.
> > He really is light."
His disciples, in awe,
> finally started to understand
> > all the words he'd told them

about his plan of victory:
suffering death,
overcoming its power,
rising from the dead,
sending his Spirit
and . . . of course . . .
the day of his powerful return.

Jesus took them aside
and reassured them that the rest of the plan
would happen just as he had promised.

"If you think your jaws are hanging open now,"
he said, "just wait!"

And then he physically
ascended
from the ground next to them.

And their jaws did drop.
And they did wait.

And several days later it happened.
Jesus sent his Spirit.

He sent his Spirit
to dwell   within
and among
his family of followers
until the day of his own
promised bodily return.

The presence of his Spirit was beyond what
they had ever imagined.

Jesus' followers knew
    that he had been right,
            so right,
     all along.
They had put their faith in the right one.

Jesus, a simple carpenter?

    Yahweh Enfleshed!
      Long-Awaited Anointed One.
       Daily Sustaining Bread.
        Friend of the Outcast.
         The Intimate Word of God.
          The Eternal Healer of Sickness.
         Embracer of Lepers.
        Sin Destroyer.
         Death Conquerer.

        Our Father.

Not a man who started a religion.

The "I Am."
The Messiah.

God come to earth to be seen in detail,

to get his feet dirty working in the grit of life,

to change the world forever.

3
Christians
Aliens!

Most folks think Christians are
harmless enough,
though a bit more boring than most.

But it turns out Jesus Followers are
by definition
neither harmless nor boring.

Responding to the Call

So, what's a Jesus Follower?

> It's common for us
> to think of a Jesus Follower
> as a religious person:
>
>> someone with high moral standards,
>> someone who lives a fairly pristine life,
>> someone with a set of dogmatic beliefs.

What a different picture Jesus gives!

> Jesus tells people the news about turning around
> and calls them to follow him.
>
>> If they follow, they are Jesus Followers.

Jesus says:
>> "I've got some good news for you . . .
>> The Kingdom of God has come near!
>>
>> You can turn around now."

> Jesus Followers are the people
> who have believed in, and responded to,
> that good news.
>
>> They've turned around!
>> And what have they turned to?
>>
>> The Kingdom of God!

A new place to live and call home.

They have been adopted into a new family,
freely granted residency in a new kingdom.

Not the Kingdom of This World.
   Not the Kingdom of Self.

      The Kingdom of God: an actual realm,
                            an order,
                            a dominion,
                            a community,
                            a nation.

According to Jesus,
      the most central descriptive of Jesus Followers
   is that they are residents of the Kingdom of God.

      They are, by definition,
            aliens to this world,
                  to their country
                        and to their home village.

      They are foreign.
      Jesus said they'd stick out
            like a thick accent,
            like torches in a dark cave.

To understand what it is to be a Jesus Follower
      we must look at this Kingdom
            and what life within its borders is like.

                  *   *   *   *

The Kingdom of God

Jesus couldn't stop talking about the Kingdom.

>He talked about it all the time.

>He usually used intriguing parables
>and provocative stories
>to describe what the Kingdom was like.

>>It was as if
>>he just couldn't quite reduce it
>>>to strict definitions
>>>or normal paradigms.

Jesus, announcing the Kingdom of God:

>>"I confer on you a kingdom!

>>You may eat and drink
>>at my royal table in my kingdom."

Jesus, after being asked when the Kingdom of God would
be coming:

>>"It's not the kind of thing
>>you can see when it comes.

>>No one will say
>>'Look, here it is!' or 'There it is!'
>>It doesn't work like that.

>>As a matter of fact,
>>this Kingdom of God

is among you.

It is within you."

Jesus, trying to wrap words around the concept of the Kingdom of God, to give folks a sense of the shape and size and heft of it:

"The Kingdom is like a buried treasure
that a man found in a field.

He sold everything he owned
and bought that field!

Again, it's like a seller of pearls
looking for fine specimens.

He finds this one pearl of such great value
that he sells everything he owns
and buys that pearl!"

Jesus, answering the unspoken questions of those around him:

"What is the Kingdom of God like?
To what should I compare it?

Well, It's like a tiny, tiny mustard seed
that someone took and sowed in the garden.

It grew and became a tree!

It got so big and strong
that the birds made nests in its branches!

To what should I compare
the Kingdom of God?

It's like the yeast
a baker mixes with flour.

It makes the loaf rise and become bread!"

* * * *

The Secret

One time Jesus talked about

"the secret of the Kingdom."

There was a huge crowd that day.
They had come to hear Jesus.
(Many were saying he was the Messiah!)
     Maybe, just maybe, they'd hear something
     about this kingdom he kept talking about.

As the immense crowd jockeyed for position,
all heads expectantly leaned toward Jesus . . .

and when he spoke,
     the words he spoke,
          the message that he had for the
               hundreds of wide-eyed faces
                    turned out to be . . .

a plain story about a farmer sowing seeds.

There was a farmer.

He sowed seeds.

Most of the seeds never grew.
Some landed on rocks.
Some were picked up by birds.
Others were choked by weeds . . .

The hero of the story was
the good soil.

The good soil received the seed,
took it in,
responded to it.

Jesus ended the story with:

"Let anyone with ears to hear listen!"

It was a simple story.
Agriculturally sound . . .

but these folks weren't interested
in an agriculture refresher course!
They wanted some religious training.
They wanted some easy answers—
at least some familiar boxes
to fit ideas into!

So most just walked away
disappointed.

But a few
were intrigued.

" . . . Seeds . . . good soil . . ."
they thought to themselves.
They didn't completely understand,
of course,
but they wanted to know more,
they wanted to respond to his teaching,
there was just something about Jesus . . .

So, against the flow of the crowd,
they decided to stick around.

And after the dust settled,
      it was just Jesus
      and these few people.

Jesus looked around at the faces
watching him with eagerness—
      faces of men and women
      who wanted to respond to what he said,
      who wanted to understand his teaching,
      who wanted to do anything but
      walk away from this Jesus.

Jesus looked around at that intimate group,
          smiled
             and said,

"You just figured out the secret, the mystery
      of the Kingdom of God."

Let anyone with ears to hear listen, indeed!

They had responded to Jesus. They had gone to him.

You see, to have a kingdom . . .
you need a king and a people.

Those are the first, central
realities of any kingdom.

Once you have a king
who will rule
and a people
who will respond to the king . .
you have a kingdom.

That's the secret of the Kingdom of God.

* * * *

The Adventure of Joining a Kingdom

The Kingdom that Jesus talked about
was a very specific Kingdom.

A Kingdom unlike any
ever experienced or read about.

Imagine a Kingdom, Jesus said, where . . .
God is the King!

What would a Kingdom like that be like?
What would it be like to live with God as King?
What would be the impact
of dwelling in that Kingdom?

The answers to those questions
were what Jesus spent most of his time talking about.

To become a Jesus Follower
>   is a giant Believing-and-Acting-on-It step:
>   it is to move in,
>>   to receive residency in the Kingdom of God,
>>>   to defect to a new nation
>>>   and build a life there.

The Kingdom Dweller has a new citizenship:
>>   no longer belonging
>>   to this world.

And the Kingdom Dweller has a new identity:
>   every citizen in the Kingdom of God
>   is named
>>   *Beloved,*
>>   *Beautiful Saint,*
>>   *Child of God.*
>   Those are the last words
>   on identity and value
>   you will ever hear in the Kingdom.

The Kingdom Dweller has a new family:
>>   Jesus called his followers
>>>   *Family,*
>>>   *Friends,*
>>>   *Beloved Children.*

The Kingdom Dweller has a new allegiance:
>   there's a change in what he or she
>>   will
>>   and will not
>>   salute.

The Kingdom Dweller has a new King:

the Kingdom of God is a monarchy
with only one royalty,
only one who'll call the shots—Jesus.

The King of Self
    and the Duke of Success
        and the Queen of Convenience
           are completely
              dethroned.

The Kingdom Dweller has a new diet:
    the Word of God is
    the bread,
    the water,
    the simple, life-sustaining fare.

The Kingdom Dweller has a new constitution
and bill of rights:
    the words of God
    are the clear pronunciation
    of reality and truth.

The Kingdom Dweller has a new relationship
with the Creator:
    Jesus sent his Spirit
    to live in and among his followers.

The Kingdom Dweller has a new perspective on life:
    because of what Jesus accomplished,
    death is no longer to be feared.

The Kingdom Dweller has a new hope in the future:
    Jesus will come back
    to fully establish his Kingdom

for eternity.

The Kingdom Dweller has a new record:
      the regrets and stains and penalties
      of a painful life of sin
      are replaced by the cleanness
      of Jesus' forgiveness.

The Kingdom Dweller has a new purpose:
      Jesus redefined greatness
      with a rag and a basin of water
          by humbly washing his disciples'
          dirty feet.
      To serve others is to live.

Moving into the Kingdom changes everything!
A whole new life—

it's almost like being born again.

*   *   *   *

A Lifetime in the Kingdom

The rebirth,
      the believing of the message in ultimate faith,
          the signing of the lease,
              the jumping over the fence in defection,
              the swearing of allegiance,
                   the moving into a new residence . . .

          this is the beginning.

The rest of the Kingdom Dweller's time on earth

is the transforming adventure of living a full life
in the new Kingdom.
The Kingdom Dweller obeys the King
and, in the process, becomes more like the King.

It is a lifetime of demanding,
                humbling,
                        beautiful,
                                risky ventures
that are worth every ounce of sweat.

Jesus' commands are life-blood.

        He likened obeying them
        to building a house on
        a solid foundation

        Obeying anything else,
                Jesus confided, is like
                        building
                        a house
                        on a
                        sandy beach . . .

        and seeing it destroyed
        in a storm.

Living under the King
and obeying his commands
builds a solid, purposeful life.

        Living by the winds of culture
                or the whims
                of personal emotion

builds a shaky, flimsy
shack.
One that will
come .
crashing
down.

Instead of following the crowds
in pursuit of money and prestige and power,

Jesus confides in his people
that true life is found
by giving one's own life away.

"Be like me.
Humbly, bravely
wash the feet of those around you,

and you will find life."

Instead of awkwardly trying to follow
the disposable morals of a given time and place,

Jesus calls his followers
to tap into true living—

living life
as Yahweh had intended it to be lived
from the beginning.

Instead of skimming along
at a superficial consumer level,

Jesus invites those in his Kingdom

into the deepest secrets of the universe,
into intimate relationship with Yahweh,

into a fully physical,
    intellectual
        and spiritual existence.

Jesus' enduring,
central message
to his followers is

"Be like me.
Live like I did.
Follow in my footsteps."

The King calls his subjects into true life,
into taking on the King's attitudes,
                  his values,
          his habits,
        his actions . . . .

The Kingdom Dweller,
with the presence of Jesus' Spirit,
is continually,
    slowly,
        truly
transformed by living life in the Kingdom.

The Kingdom of God:
    A life of devotion to a King,
        allegiance to a Kingdom,
            rebirth into a family,
                a new name–*Beloved*.

These Jesus Followers,
these Kingdom Dwellers . . .
    they're illegal aliens,
        foreign ambassadors,
            a threat to national security
in their blatant devotion to another Kingdom!

Instead of yawning
    and waving these Jesus Followers aside
        as harmless
        and a bit boring,

    we should feel tempted to call the FBI!

4
Repentance
180 Degrees

Most folks think repentance is about
sitting remorsefully in the corner.

But it turns out it's impossible to repent
while sitting down.

Choreography, Not Apology

When Jesus sat down with people
and told them the good news about his Kingdom,

> he would encourage them to "repent"
> and believe in that Kingdom.

> > But despite the modern use of the term,
> > Jesus was not saying   "have regret" or
> >   "feel bad" or
> >   "embrace remorse."

> Far from it.

> The word *repentance* is not about
> > > heavy shoulders
> > > or guilty consciences
> > > or averting eyes
> > > > out of shame.

> No.

> Repentance is an active and hopeful way of life!

To "repent" is, literally,
> to stop,
> to turn around,
> and to head in the other direction.

It is more a thing of the playing field
than of the support group,
> more about dancing on the dance floor
> than sitting in the corner.

In *The Adventures of the Jesus Followers*,
     repentance is, specifically, the act of
     stopping your life,
          turning around,
               and walking straight
               into the outrageous
               Kingdom of God,

               into the arms of a father
                    who knows
                         and understands
                              and forgives.
Repentance is

     to stop   in your tracks,
                  admitting you're going
                  the wrong way,
                  believing that there is a better way,

     to turn   from the kingdom of the world,
                  the kingdom of sin,
                  the kingdom of self
                  (whatever holds sway
                  over your life),

     and to walk straight into the open arms
                  of this Kingdom's
                  Father-King.

                         (No one is turned away.)

          *   *   *   *

The Need to Turn

Repentance assumes we are going the wrong way.

> This is either the most disconcerting
> > or the most honestly refreshing
> > > fact
> > > about repentance.

> Repentance is the beginning of the Jesus Follower,
> and failure is the beginning of repentance.

> > In fact, all of
> > *The Adventures of the Jesus Followers*
> > are based upon
> > and consistently assume
> > human failure.

> The centrality of repentance
> within *The Adventures of the Jesus Followers*
> clearly illustrates that in "Christianity" we have
> > no high, ethereal, esoteric philosophy,
> > no blow-a-little-sunshine smiley-face religion,
> > no militaristic academy of moral perfection,
> > no affirming spirits or nicely vague spirituality.

No.
The Adventures,
> > in their example of repentance as a way of life,
> > clearly demonstrate that
> > we live difficult,
> > > mean,
> > > > aimless,
> > > > > complicated
> > > > and otherwise cumbersome lives.

To be human is to stumble.

To be human is to be selfish and insecure.

To be human is to live in fear of death.

To be human is to think shoving
   fistfuls of rocks in our mouths
   will satisfy our hunger.

This is the foundation of *The Adventures:*

   Humanity is terminally broken.

* * * *

The Beauty of Turning

Jesus Followers know that
the truest diagnosis of reality is
                              "fallen."

   But they also know that's not the last word.

   Jesus Followers assume reality,
   but they believe in and celebrate the good news that

      brokenness doesn't have to reign!

You see, Jesus claimed he had won a huge victory.

   By beating death.

   Jesus made all sorts of new things possible

for his children,
for those who put their faith in him,
who enter the Kingdom he's King over,
who believe there really is
some good news!

To be human is to be broken,
hungry,
aimless
and insecure.
But to repent and believe
is to enter a Kingdom of balm,
bread,
purpose—
and to be called Beloved.

That Kingdom was the good news
Jesus walked around announcing:

"You can turn around now!
The Kingdom of beauty and change is here."

There is a place where pains and wounds
don't have to be politely covered up—

they are healed.

There is a place where mistakes
don't have to be justified or ignored—

they are forgiven.

There is a place where value
doesn't have to be fought for

or purchased—

it is given
by a loving Father.

There is a place where blindness
and aimless fumbling
don't have to be settled for—

they are set right
by the Good Shepherd.

There is a place where death
doesn't have to be feared—

it is merely a threshold.

The initial taste
of repentance can be shocking—humility
is anything but
commonplace.

But the sweeter
more enduring taste
is one of utter freedom and hope.

To repent is to stop
and turn, in faith, to Jesus and his Kingdom
for wisdom,
healing,
understanding,
right living
and sustenance.

Repentance is beautiful

because it assumes brokenness and longing and fumbling

and (because of Jesus)
it ends in healing and satisfaction and direction

Broken lives are transformed
by the repentance Jesus offered.

* * * *

A Life of Turning

It turns out
pledging one's life to the King, Jesus,
is good for humans.

It has a healing effect.
His tasks are a balm

In his Kingdom
humanity is not erased or ignored.

Humanity works out!
Practices.
Ever stumbling,
ever repenting,
ever growing . . .

The Kingdom is a training ground
for those willing to enter its boundaries
(thereby admitting their need for training).

When the bulky, cumbersome backpack
of hopelessness and regret

is removed,

backs can straighten again,
eyes don't have to be averted anymore,
folks start feeling light and agile—
ready to start training!

Painfully forced postures of

Togetherness and Satisfaction and Perfection

are no longer necessary.

Repentance is an alternative to pretending.

It is an invitation to grow.

It is the national motto
of the Kingdom of God.

It is running into the arms
of a loving Father.

It's the best dance
you'll ever boogie to.

It truly is *freedom*.

5
Church
The Tribe

Most folks think church is an old building
with plenty of stained glass
and straight wooden pews.

But it turns out calling a church a building
is like calling a Jesus Follower a two-by-four.

Us

All of those steepled buildings you see around town?
    Turns out none of them are churches.
    (Those signs out front certainly are misleading!)

    It turns out that church has never been a building.
    Church is all those Kingdom Dwellers put together.

The plural of "Jesus Follower" is "church."

        It's nothing but a fancy way
        for Jesus Followers to say
            "we" or "us."

But church isn't a chance happening.

    It isn't merely a fluke
        that more than one person
            happened to follow Jesus.

    Church is not an occurrence.

    It is the design.

Jesus never meant for his disciples to be alone.

The first thing Jesus did to start his ministry
was to call his disciples together.

    Jesus went everywhere together with his disciples.
    When he did send them out, it was at least in pairs.

        "Where two or more are gathered

in my name [when it's plural]," he said,
"I am there with them."

Jesus prayed for the plural—
that "we" would always remain
together.

The Jesus Follower rarely needs the words

    "I" or "me"

in his or her vocabulary.

Jesus insisted there is a Plural Imperative:
    Church is disciples following together.

Yahweh has always been clear
that he doesn't live in
buildings built by humans.

Those steepled contraptions?
    Those are just how the church gets out of the rain.

*   *   *   *

The First Us

After Jesus had sent his promised Spirit to his followers,
    that gregarious fisherman, Peter,
        spoke about the good news
            and three thousand people
                believed the good news,
                    crossed the border
                        and became Jesus Followers.

When those three thousand joined the Kingdom,
the Us was so amazing
that someone wrote down
all the plural things that were happening:

"All the new Kingdom Dwellers devote themselves
        to each other,
            to the words of the earliest citizens,
                to prayer
                    and to eating bread together
                    (to remember their Bread, Jesus.)

"An awe comes upon everyone
        because of the power
        the Jesus Followers have.

"They are all together;
        They have all things in common;
        They go and sell what they own
            and give the money
            to whoever needs it!

"They daily meet together in the Jewish temple,
        they go from house to house
        breaking loaves of bread and eating them
        (like Jesus told them to)
            and whenever they eat
            they are glad
            and very sincere about it!

"They can't help but talk about
how great their God, Yahweh, is.
        And everyone can't help but notice
        and be attracted to them.

"And every day they grow in numbers!"

This was the earliest church,
> the first plural followers,
>> the first Us.

Church: A bunch of Kingdom Dwellers following Jesus.
           (Steeples and pews not included.)

* * * *

Changed by Us

Jesus seemed convinced
that being one of these human-being types is all about
> loving others
> and being loved.

> In fact,
> being with others is so key,
>> so central to everything,
>>> that he didn't offer some private,
>>> individualistic religion.
> No.
>> Jesus formed,
>> he gathered
>>> a Kingdom of people.

The stuff of the Kingdom of God . . .

> seeing brokenness and repenting,
>> talking with Yahweh,
>>> being named Valuable and Beloved,
>>>> loving and serving others as Jesus did,

obeying the King . . .
should be done with others.

It just works that way, he insisted.

There is something rehabilitating,
something deeply cleansing,
something inherently right

about men and women and kids throwing
their lot in with others
as they all together respond
to Jesus' "Follow me."

From very early on in the church,
a striking thing happened:
These Jesus Followers
started calling each other   brother,
sister,
mother,
father . . .

The church is both a kingdom

and a family
of Jesus Followers.

There's something about doggedly pursuing Jesus,
about living in his Kingdom,
that transforms and draws folks together
like nothing else.

* * * *

Leading Us

The church is people.
    People mess up.
        Therefore the church needs help!

Jesus knew this and asked Peter
            (three times)
    to help take care of the church.

"Care for my people, Peter.
        Tend my sheep, Peter.
            And follow me."

Peter was the perfect one for the job.
He knew messing up inside and out!
Even so, Jesus had renamed him
        the Rock
        and then made him
    a sheep-who-shepherds.

    Jesus asked Peter to serve,
                to give
                    and to lead
    as he himself followed Jesus.

Peter, then, called all Jesus Followers
    sheep-who-shepherd.

    All citizens of God's nation mess up,
            and so all citizens of God's nation
                must pick up the rag and water basin
                    to serve
                        and give

and lead.

The church is people helping each other follow Jesus.
The herd's mistakes are well documented,
inside and outside Scripture.

Lots of shepherding is needed.

And so the sheep themselves do some shepherding—
strongly leading,
    humbly serving,
        and always following after Jesus.

* * * *

Still Us

The church is a family of folks
for whom death is a non-issue.

Eternal living sure makes for a huge family!

There are no churches.
There is only church.

One church.

Sure, there are a number of buildings
that shelter Jesus Followers from the elements,

and there are a number of names
posted on those buildings . . .
but there is only one church, one family.

Every single Jesus Follower
counts all the other Jesus Followers
as brothers
and sisters.

Sure, there are sibling rivalries,
as one would expect.

But there's only one family
because there's only one Father.

All are pluralized,
brought together in the arms of the Father,
no matter where on earth they live
or when on earth they lived.

The church is a great nation, with a grand tradition.
(Our neighbors who are Jesus Followers
have joined quite a family!)

The church:
old buildings with uncomfortable pews
and countless altars?
No.

An immense nation!
A worldwide family of devoted followers
from every age,
every race,
every country imaginable!

Talk about diversity!

It is nearly unfathomable, this family of Jesus Followers.

6
Prayer
Blue-Collar Spirituality

Most folks think prayer is the quiet work
of barefoot monks with brown hoods
in some faraway land.

But it turns out prayer
has more to do with your own bedroom
than with some distant monastery.

A Shocking Possibility

Jesus assumed that in prayer
awkward, fragile Jesus Followers
commune with the Creator of the universe

> Prayer is great disparity
> being reconciled.

>> Tiny humans
>> (who aren't always
>> that impressive
>> when they look
>> in the mirror
>> in the morning)

>>> and the "I Am"
>>> (whose bountiful largess
>>> dwarfs entire galaxies
>>> with a mere eyelash)

> come together!

A ludicrous conversation made quite possible.

> Broken humans and a holy and perfect God
> talking.

It's so ludicrous,
so far-fetched
> that it takes faith
> to even believe it's possible.

> But that's exactly what Jesus insisted it was:

possible.

Sure, it's ludicrous:
    Like swallowing the Nile River.

    Like holding
    the oceans' deeps and all their
    dark water and life and mystery in one hand.

    Like inhaling New York City!

But, according to Jesus,
    it's a conversation that's
        enjoyable,
            satisfying,
                comfortable . .

        and, yes, quite possible

* * * *

At Home

Jesus had this to say to his followers about prayer

    "And when you pray
    don't be like the hypocrites
        who love to use prayer
        as a performance.
        They are concerned
        with their prayers
        being heard by other people, not God.

    When you pray

be at home.
Be intimate.

And pray to your Father
who is sitting
in your room with you
where you are praying.

"When you pray don't heap up empty phrases.
Folks who think they'll be heard
because of their many words
are wrong.

Don't be like them.

"Instead, pray like this:

our Father in heaven

may your name be lifted
as holy and different

may your Kingdom come

may your will be done here on earth
just like it is in heaven

give us today our bread for the day

forgive our sins
as we too forgive others

protect us from temptation
and rescue us from the enemy."

Prayer is no rare, fancy-worded performance.
It's a daily family conversation.
It's simple.

* * * *

Warts and All

Pretense is not prayer,
it's a waste of time.

> The point is communion,
> > conversation with God.

> Not impressing God.

Jesus told this story:

> "Two men went up to church to pray.

> "One was a religious leader,
> and the other a shady collector
> > of oppressive taxes.

> "The religious leader
> stood by himself and said,
> > 'God, thank you that I am
> > > > obviously
> > > not like other people:
> > > > thieves,
> > > > > rogues,
> > > > > > adulterers
> > > > or even this tax collector.
> > > > I fast twice a week . . .

I give a tenth of all my income
to the church.'

"The shady
tax collector
stood far off.

"He wouldn't even look up to heaven.

"He was beating
his breast, saying,
'God, be merciful to me, a sinner!'

"I tell you,
this man went down to his home
having been with God.

"The religious leader did not."

Prayer is not an attempt to impress,
it is a time to finally relax and be honest.

*   *   *   *

Body Language

Folded-Hands-and-Closed-Eyes
is not the mandatory posture for prayer.

Praying isn't necessarily calm and sedate
for a Jesus Follower.

It is . . . it is a real child
interacting with the real Father.

Posture isn't something to be forced,

it is to reflect a person's interaction with God.

Prayer can be
as aerobic
as it is contemplative,

as angry
as it is thankful.

The Bible is full of accounts of folks
bowing,
dancing,
crying,
raising hands . .
all in prayer!

Once, while Jesus was praying,
his sweat
became like great
drops
of blood
falling down on the ground!

If someone's confused,
they should ask questions!

If they're angry,
there should be yelling!

Whether said while kneeling beside a bed,
walking along a street,
driving on the freeway

or taking a morning shower,

prayer is to be genuine.

There is no prerequisite posture.

It is a child and a Father, talking.

* * * *

Prayer Is Amen

Sometimes prayers end
with a little word: "Amen."

That tiny word
holds a big meaning:

So Be It!
Let It Be So!
Make It So!

So, prayer is not passive.

Prayer is never therapy,
distraction,
catharsis
or wishful thinking.

It is inherently active
and productive.

Jesus insisted that prayer actually works.
He told this story:

"There was an evil judge
who hated people and God.

Suffice it to say,
he was not easily swayed!

"But, if he was bugged enough,
he would grant anything to anyone . .
just because he was fed up!

"If even jerks respond this way,"
Jesus reasoned,
"Then how much more
will a loving, powerful, intimate
Father-God

quickly respond
to the prayers
of his precious people?"

Of course prayer works, Jesus insisted.

It is faith expressed.

It is blue-collar spirituality.

It is a hug from a father
and a construction crew meeting
all in one.

It is a classroom.
And the subject is reality.

Prayer accomplishes.
Prayer is the ridiculous being born.

Like moving Mount Everest with a word.

7
The Bible
Dripping Pages

Most folks insist that the Bible
is an outdated old book

But it turns out that usually
they've never actually read the thing.

Books Are for Reading

Let's be honest.

    The Bible's reputation,
        whether "Infallible & Holy!"
        or "Fabricated & Outdated!"
    invariably precedes the book itself.

    Sure, we want to come
    to some personal conclusions
    about this famous book,
        but in our laziness
        and credulity
    we vaguely flip through its thin, gold-edged pages
    relying more on the set of preconceived notions
    we happen to have selected as our own
        than on the various texts themselves.

The Bible is perhaps the most talked-about book
no one's ever read.

    Searching for and memorizing
    pithy, comforting passages from its pages
    is not reading.

    Scouring its sentences for apparent contradictions
    is not reading.

    The Bible was intended
    to be neither a logical proof
        nor a pleasant,
        thickly-shellacked
        bathroom hanging.

It has been called a love letter. And it's written to us.

* * * *

Romantic Wrestling Match

The Bible is the long-reaching,
            epic account
            of a people and their God,
            of a God and his people.

   The book covers
   thousands of years of relationship
         between this people, Israel,
         and this God, Yahweh.

   "Israel" literally means "wrestles with God,"
         and that certainly describes
               the color
                  and tenor
                     and subject matter of the Bible.

The epic story of this wrestling is told like no other.

   It is a common misconception
   that the Bible
   is predictably stocked with smooth, religious words;
         is the stuff of lengthy hymns,
                  dry, crusty histories,
                      irrelevant laws
                         and a mouthful of
                            "thees" and "thous."

   The fact is

folks from around the world
and throughout the centuries
have been utterly stunned
by the brash contents of this book.

In the Bible we have
an unlikely romantic wrestling match

between Yahweh and his people.

The Bible is the colorful biography
of a people wrestling with Yahweh

And the medium for this story?   No smooth,
appropriate
religious
words.

Instead we find
scandalous,
image-filled,
sharply cutting,
specific and earthy,
meaty words.

The pages of the Bible are so loaded they drip!

Tear-soaked poems,
detailed histories,
shocking prophetic sermons,
real-life survival accounts,
truth-engulfing wisdom,
desperate blood-stained prayers,
revealing love letters,

passionate dancing songs,
murders . . .
these are what crowd the pages of the Bible!

A people and their God.

These people—
they praise their God,
yell at him,
mess with him,
deny him,
repent and go back to him,
introduce their children to him,
despair while forgetting him,
put their faith in him,
sing songs to him,
seek and obey him,
admire him—

And this God,
he comforts his people,
speaks truth to them,
woos them,
reveals reality to them,
gives promises to them,
redeems them,
saves them,
holds and feeds and teaches them.

Anyone who tries to peek,

who dares open the pages of Scripture,

will find no smooth religious phraseology,

but a plethora
of meaty words
to chew on and contemplate.
Words that satisfy.
Words so loaded, they drip.

* * * * *

He Is Who He Is

It must be admitted
that the strange ancient Israelites
had an even stranger God.

He called himself
"I am what I am"
and was so unlike
any other "gods" around

that Israel quickly recognized him
as the only true God—

and just as quickly began asking him
the all-important (and brave)
question:

"If 'You are what you are,'
then . . .
well . . .
what are you?!"

If this utterly unique God
isn't like all those silly
fertility dolls and bull statues,

then what *is* he like?

The pages of the Bible record Yahweh's answer to that question.

> The Bible reveals this Yahweh;
> his voice resonates deeply throughout every page.

> His self-disclosure,
>   his divine wisdom,
>   his tender words of love . . .
> all find a crystal-clear pronunciation
> in the pages of Scripture.

Is there any rhyme or reason to the course of history?
 Is it possible to reconcile old, bitter problems?
  Why is there so much pain in the world?
   Is there anything to hope in or trust?
    What's the nature of God, after all?
     What's all imbedded in creation?
      Is there truth that can be known?
       Why do my relationships sour?
        How do I find joy, real joy?
         Is forgiveness a possibility?
          What does God do for fun?
           What's the point of it all?
            What happens after I die?
             Does God know I exist?
              Why should I care?
               Where is God?
                Does he care?
                 Real truth?
                  Where?
                   Who?

Why?

Throughout the centuries
    Yahweh Wrestlers and Jesus Followers,
      men and women and children,
        Russians and Chileans and Greeks,
          farmers and kings and beggars,
            the angry and sad and ecstatic,
              the strong and weak and dying . . .

have all independently looked to one book for answers.

    And they say that they not only have found answers
    but have encountered there the voice of God,

    the Word of God.

*   *   *   *

Read the Thing

It would seem that the Bible is the most
    generation-spanning,
      literarily diverse,
        interest-piqueing,
          soul-searching,
            mind-edifying,
              life-clarifying
  message
  ever recorded.

    But don't take anyone's word for it.
    Refuse to swallow any summary,
        critique,

        praise
        or description of the Bible.

Curiously explore its diverse landscapes.

    Deeply delve into its various mysteries.

        Slowly comb through the age-old promises.

    The path of least resistance
        is to nod
        in unison with   whatever opinion
                        finds itself most popular
                        in your vicinity.
    The path of integrity
        is to investigate
        and discover the book for yourself.

Let's face it: The quickest and most dependable way
    to get beyond
    the stereotypes
    and clichés about the Bible

    is to read the thing.

    It has 66 books in two sections.
    The Old Testament has 39 books.
    The New Testament, 27.

We could sit in our pile of inherited assumptions.
Or we could go see.

8
Salvation
Grassy Feast

Most folks think of salvation
as some sort of heavenly retirement package or
comprehensive hell-avoidance insurance policy.

But it turns out salvation
is more like an extravagant banquet
that's being served right now.

Abundant Care

Salvation, it's often assumed,
    is the shiny halo and wings we earn
    by not smoking or cussing here on earth.

Now, Yahweh's always been into salvation—
    it's what he does for a living!

    But this salvation was never conceived of
        as some sort of far-off spiritual retirement
    or heavenly private country club,
        with only the elite admitted.

    Salvation was always real
        and tangible
            and immediate
                and essential
                    and earthy
                        and generous.

    The original Hebrew word
    for salvation is *yesa*.

    It literally means
    "to bring to a spacious environment."
    It is an active, present-tense word.

        When a bearded
        Hebrew shepherd
        guided his sheep

            toward new grasses
            and clear, fresh waters

and away from
hungry wolves
and steep-edged cliffs,

he was literally
providing *salvation*
for those sheep.

To *save* was to

powerfully,
gently,
wisely,
proactively
shepherd.

So when these bearded Hebrews
heard their God, Yahweh, say

"I am your Savior,"

they knew exactly what he meant.

He would lead them,
    he would protect them,
        and, no matter what,
    he would provide abundantly for them.

This saving nature of Yahweh
was so central that *God* and *Savior*
eventually became
interchangeable words.

Who was God?

He was the one that
    extravagantly and wisely
    led
    and protected
    and provided for them.

Yahweh—from the very beginning and still today—
is the one who brings salvation.

       *   *   *   *

The Family Business

Yahweh's ultimate plan for saving his people
involved Jesus from the beginning.

    As the Messiah,
    God Enfleshed,
        Jesus would come as the decisive,
                strong,
                    steady,
                        ultimate
        provider of salvation,

    the final hero of the Great Rescue Mission.

    Jesus' birth
    was predicted
    as the birth of
        "one who will save his people."

The name
Jesus
literally means

"Yahweh is salvation."

As Jesus walked those dusty streets
saying he came "to save"

> those words rang
> with deep resonance
> in the ears of those he spoke to.

The God who had always
brought his people into a spacious environment

had come, in Jesus,

with the extravagant news of repentance
that would lead people to full and abundant life.

> Jesus was, indeed, the Good Shepherd—

> the Best of Shepherds.

> Jesus' message of salvation
> was richly saturated with meaning
> for its hearers.

> They could actually taste and smell and see
> what he was saying.

Salvation was a sheep being brought to green pastures.

> Salvation was seeing those intimidating,
> slobbering, fanged wolves simply wiped away.

> Salvation was being offered life.

And not just any life:
> an amazing,
> abundant,
> cup-overflowing life.

"Salvation"

> is another way of saying

"being offered a lavish, unbelievable life
as an alternative to death."

* * * *

Three Small Words

Salvation has always been a beautiful thing.

And it has always been immensely unpopular.

> Salvation implies need.

> A *savior* (by definition)
> isn't something people merely desire
> or opt for
> or settle for.

> A savior is someone who is
> utterly,
> > desperately,
> > > fully *needed*.

Jesus was always clear about this.

Very early on he clarified his purpose:

"Those who are well
    have no need
    of a physician,

    but those who are sick
    do.

"I have come
    to call   not the righteous
                   but sinners."

Just as repentance assumes
people are facing the wrong way,

so salvation assumes
people need to be saved.

        It's simply logical.   And very
                                  uncomfortable.

Over and over and over Jesus' repeated,
                              steady
                                  message
                                      was:
                              "You need me."

You need me.

    Jesus' parables and teachings
    were utterly saturated
    with this one simple message:

    You are lost, dull sheep. And I am a shepherd.

You are blind. And I am a healer of eyes.

You are stumbling in darkness. And I am light.

You are branches. And I am the life-connecting vine.

You are starving. And I am bread.

You are dying of thirst. And I am water.

You are on a journey.   And I am the path to,
                                    and the gate for,
                                    your final destination.

Jesus knew that   by being killed
                                    and not staying dead

he would change reality forever
for those   who would respond to his news,
                    following him
                    and entering his Kingdom.

He knew he could offer life.

        He knew that after seeing him alive again
                people would
                stand
                wide-eyed
                and breathe,

        "We really *do* need you."

So, in a steady, compassionate voice,
        in his life and in his words,

>   he confided
>   continually,

"You need me.

"I come offering life.
You are sheep.
And I am the one who can shepherd you."

It's no wonder
he was embraced
by those who knew their needful condition,

>   and rejected and fought
>   by those who felt
>   they could get along just fine,
>   thank you very much!

* * * *

The Nature of the Feast

Jesus made it very clear
that the salvation he came with

>   was not some sort of
>   cut-rate spacious environment.

"Yes, you desperately need life,"
          he assured people.

"But this life is abundant,
          is extravagant,
                    is fruitful,

is powerful,
is joyful—
is a feast!"

Jesus didn't come offering
bare-minimum rations
to a dying people.

He came offering
an amazing, opulent, lavish, unending feast
to a dying people.

That is the nature
of how he provides for his followers.
Abundantly.

But his amazing offer of life went even further!

You see, Jesus assumed eternity.

He spoke of death never as an end,
but as a threshold.

"You are not just temporary
collections of chemicals.
You are not accidents," he insisted.

"You are designed and intended
to last forever.

"You were created to live, not to die."

Jesus was clear that death is a threshold
to one of two places:

either an eternity with God
or an eternity apart from God.

While Jesus was utterly concerned
with people's lives on earth,
offering to shepherd them into abundant life,

he was equally concerned with them
once their few days on earth were ended,
offering to shepherd them into eternal life.

As the Good Shepherd
who had himself defeated death,
       Jesus could lead
       all those who would follow him
          right
              through
                  the valley of death
               to the eternal green pastures that lay beyond.

His concern
and his salvation
     were always full,
     always comprehensive,
     always taking into account the
                 reality
                 and sureness
                 of eternity.

Having overcome even death,
Jesus was in the unique position
to say in a sure voice,

    "I have life for you.

Life abundant.
And life eternal."

* * * *

Not a Popular Answer

What a beautiful message.

Jesus offers abundant life.
Eternal life.

He will wisely and bountifully shepherd
all who will come to him.

But for many, what a frustrating message!

If Jesus had stopped at saying simply
"You need . . ."
he would have angered many!

But he went so much further
by adding one little word: "me."
"If you want life,"
he confided,
"you should come to the one who has it—me."

Oh my!

Jesus' simple message of salvation,
"I am the one who can give life,
life more abundant than you've ever imagined,
life that does not end at death,"

flew in the face
of every existing philosophy
and belief system
of his day.

It would be silly to allow our
enlightened third-millennium pride
to falsely tell us that salvation,
        while a popular concept in
        Jesus' "superstitious age,"
is useless to us "enlightened ones."

His message found enemies and ridiculers
the moment it reached human ears.

Those who didn't see their need were indignant.

The seemingly content,
the self-satisfied,
the proud—
        all insisted they were completely fine.

"That Jesus is ridiculous! Hunger?!
                Thirst?!
            Darkness?!
        A lost sheep?!!!
Give me a break. I feel fine!"

These folks laughed at nearly everything Jesus said.

And those who didn't have a problem admitting they
        were in desperate need but felt they already
        had the answer elsewhere,
                were enraged.

The Greeks studiously sought out wisdom.
    They believed that attaining
    some secret,
                        esoteric knowledge
    would be their salvation.

        (They hated it when Jesus said we must all
        be like little children in order to be saved.)

The Jewish religious leaders carefully focused on law.
    They relied on strict adherence to specific
    rabbinic codes and laws to earn their salvation.

        (They hated it when Jesus said a life
        full of good—even miraculous!— deeds
        couldn't save anything.)

The Romans achieved social order.
    They structured their city-states
    to politically attain liberty,
    and everything else there was need for!

        (Those Romans hated it when Jesus made
        the bald statement that being saved
        is absolutely impossible for people
        by themselves—regardless of how strong
        and organized their social efforts.)

The mystery cults crafted rituals.
    They insisted that experiencing
    an ecstatic, emotional ceremony
    would take care of everything.

> (They hated Jesus' insistence
> that real, true saving work
> takes place inside of people.)

There's no question that many people in Jesus' day
hated his simple, outrageous claim:

> "I have life for you."

And people haven't stopped hating it since.

*   *   *   *

Responding to Jesus

Jesus was loved.
And Jesus was hated.

> People either
> gladly dropped
> everything
> to follow him,
>
> > or they spat in disgust
> > and plotted his murder.

His words were too clear,
    his life too stunning,
        his actions too miraculous

    for those who saw him and his dirty feet
    to respond in any other way.

Jesus' salvation is either

a beautiful invitation
to an amazing Kingdom,

a generous, earthy, eternal
offer of abundant life

that should so compel us

that we drop
our familiar nets

and follow him,

> or it is a brash,
> arrogant,
> insulting lie
>
> that should
> disgust us
>
> and disqualify
> Jesus forever
>
> as any sort of decent,
> well-meaning moral teacher.

Either way, it clearly has nothing to do
     with earning a halo and wings
     by not smoking or cussing!

And it clearly demands a response.

Afterword

In the end it would seem that the bulky legacy of stereotypes and clichés we've received about Jesus and Jesus Followers doesn't serve us very well.

Trying to come to some conclusion about Jesus just from stereotypes about him is a bit like trying to decide whether or not to go to the Grand Canyon when all we've ever seen is a grainy etch-a-sketch doodle of it.

Once most of the misleading, inexact doodles are stripped away and we take a simple look at Jesus himself and the life he offers, we are in a much better place to form an accurate opinion of him. My hope is that this book has been a bit helpful in getting you closer to that place.

I myself grew up utterly saturated with stereotypes and clichés about Jesus. I knew all those assumptions about him backwards and forwards. And I gave those assumptions a logical response: utter disinterest on most days, vague sentimentality on the holidays.

What a chilling day when I first got an unfettered glimpse of Jesus. I realized I had never responded to *him*—only to the assumptions I had about him.

And there he was, with dirty feet and a little smile on his face, seemingly staring at me. He was much more interesting and unsettling than I had ever assumed. The life he offered was much more dangerous and countercultural than I had ever heard.

And for the first time I was in a place where I could honestly reject Jesus and his misled followers every where—or truly call out to him.

It is that kind of honest, reality-based decision that I hope this book has taken you closer to, whatever your final conclusions may be.

May the real you respond to the real Jesus.

Biblical References

The picture of Jesus given in these pages has come from the four books called "Gospels" (*gospel* means, appropriately, "good news"). Individually titled Matthew, Mark, Luke and John, they are first-hand accounts of the life of Jesus.

While a careful reading of one of the Gospels in its entirety is the best way to continue to learn about Jesus, it may be helpful for you to look up some of the texts (from these Gospels and a few other books of the Bible) specifically referenced or paraphrased throughout this book.

1 Christianity: *Smelly Fishermen*
Mark 1:16 *(Simon and Andrew)*
Mark 1:17 *(follow me)*
Mark 3:14-19 *(list of disciples)*
Mark 16:15-16 *(Great Commission)*
Acts 9:2 *("People of the Way")*
Acts 11:26 *("Christians")*

2 Jesus: *God's Dirty Feet*
Luke 2:46-47 *(awed rabbis)*
Mark 10:13-16 *(children with Jesus)*
Luke 7:36-38 *(prostitutes)*
Luke 20:39-40 *(expert debaters)*
Mark 1:9 *(baptize)*
Matthew 4:1-11 *(wilderness)*
Mark 1:28 *(intrigued people)*
Mark 3:6 *(panicked leaders)*
Mark 1:41 *(leper)*
Exodus 3:14 *("I Am")*

Luke 2:25-35 *(Simeon)*
Mark 1:14-15 *(turn around)*
Mark 1:17 *(follow me)*
John 6:35, 53-58 *(bread)*
John 8:12 *(light)*
John 10:11-15 *(sheep)*
John 15:1-6 *(vine)*
Luke 15:11-32 *(Father)*
Mark 10:32-34 *(strategy)*
Luke 12:40 *(promised return)*
Luke 24:51 *(ascending)*
John 14:26 *(promised Spirit)*
Acts 2 *(sent Spirit)*

3 Christians: *Aliens!*
Matthew 5:13-16 *(stick out)*
Luke 22:29-30 *(confer Kingdom)*
Luke 17:20-21 *(Kingdom among you)*
Matthew 13:44-46 *(treasure, pearl)*
Luke 13:18-21 *(mustard seed, leaven)*
Mark 4:3-11 *(secret of Kingdom)*
Luke 13:26 *(coming back)*
John 13:1-17 *(washing dirty feet)*
Luke 6:47-49 *(house on rock)*

4 Repentance: *180 Degrees*
Mark 1:15 *(repent)*
Luke 15:11-32 *(arms of father)*

5 Church: *The Tribe*
Mark 3:13-19 *(calling of disciples)*
Mark 6:7 *(sent in pairs)*
Matthew 18:20 *(two or more)*
John 17:20-23 *(praying for plural)*
Acts 2:33 *(Spirit sent, Peter preaches)*
Acts 2:41-47 *(first Us)*
Mark 3:31 *(family)*

John 21:15-17 *(feed my sheep)*
1 Peter 2:5-10 *(all are pastors)*

6 Prayer: *Blue-Collar Spirituality*
Matthew 6:5-13 *(when you pray)*
Luke 18:10-14 *(Pharisee and tax man)*
Luke 22:43-44 *(sweating blood)*
Luke 18:1-8 *(jerky judge)*

8 Salvation: *Grassy Feast*
Luke 19:9 *(Jesus came to save)*
Matthew 1:21 *(Jesus' birth)*
Acts 11:18 *(repentance leading to life)*
John 10:11 *(Good Shepherd)*
Mark 2:17 *(sick and well)*
John 10:11-15 *(sheep)*
John 8:12 *(light)*
John 15:1-6 *(vine)*
John 6:35 *(bread)*
John 7:37-38 *(water)*
John 14:6 *(path, gate)*
John 10:10 *(abundant life)*
John 3:15 *(eternal life)*
Mark 10:13-16 *(be like children)*
Matthew 7:21-23 *(miraculous life can't save)*
Luke 18:26 *(impossible for mortals)*
Mark 7:14-15 *(inside work)*